Parenting Teens

Parenting With Love and Logic Way to Tame a Strong-willed Child

(The Inspiring Danish Way to Raise Independent, Empathic and Happy Kids)

Peter Jackson

Published by Rob Miles

© **Peter Jackson**

All Rights Reserved

Parenting Teens: Parenting With Love and Logic Way to Tame a Strong-willed Child (The Inspiring Danish Way to Raise Independent, Empathic and Happy Kids)

ISBN 978-1-990084-24-9

All rights reserved. No part of this guide may be reproduced in any form without permission in writing from the publisher except in the case of brief quotations embodied in critical articles or reviews.

Legal & Disclaimer

The information contained in this book is not designed to replace or take the place of any form of medicine or professional medical advice. The information in this book has been provided for educational and entertainment purposes only.

The information contained in this book has been compiled from sources deemed reliable, and it is accurate to the best of the Author's knowledge; however, the Author cannot guarantee its accuracy and validity and cannot be held liable for any errors or omissions. Changes are periodically made to this book. You must consult your doctor or get professional medical advice before using any of the suggested remedies, techniques, or information in this book.

Upon using the information contained in this book, you agree to hold harmless the Author from and against any damages, costs, and expenses, including any legal fees potentially resulting from the application of any of the information provided by this guide. This disclaimer applies to any damages or injury caused by the use and application, whether directly or indirectly, of any advice or information presented, whether for breach of contract, tort, negligence, personal injury, criminal intent, or under any other cause of action.

You agree to accept all risks of using the information presented inside this book.

You need to consult a professional medical practitioner in order to ensure you are both able and healthy enough to participate in this program.

Table of Contents

INTRODUCTION 1

CHAPTER 1: THE GREATEST GIFT – YOUR CHILD 3

CHAPTER 2: NUTRITION 9

CHAPTER 3: DEVELOPING MORAL VALUES AND CONSCIOUS PARENTING 19

CHAPTER 4: KIDS AND GADGETS 30

CHAPTER 5: EFFECTIVE POSITIVE PARENTING TIPS 48

CHAPTER 6: WHAT MAKES PARENTING SEEM PROBLEMATIC? 58

CHAPTER 7: PARENTS NEED TO AGREE ON PARENTING ... 64

CHAPTER 8: HOW YOU SHAPE YOUR BABY'S BRAIN 69

CHAPTER 9: WORKING ON YOURSELF TO BECOME A BETTER PARENT 85

CHAPTER 10: DISCIPLINE: WHAT TYPE OF PARENT ARE YOU? 100

CHAPTER 11: TAKING CARE OF YOURSELF 109

CHAPTER 12: DOES IT MAKE SENSE TO PRAISE A CHILD OFTEN? 126

CHAPTER 13: RESPECT 130

CHAPTER 14: PATIENT PARENTING 139

CHAPTER 15: KNOW THY CHILD 158

CHAPTER 16: SELF-ESTEEM, THE GREAT MISUNDERSTANDING 163

CONCLUSION 180

Introduction

This book will teach you how to raise kids as a sole parent. There are a number of reasons why most end up as part of a sole parent family. It may be because of divorce or the death of a partner. Isolation, financial problems, loneliness, and sometimes, aggravation from the absent partner are just some of the things being confronted by a sole parent. It may be tough for single parents, but remember that you have choices in the course you take, whereas the children are not so fortunate. They have no say about the situation and just remain stuck with something that is out of their control.

If you are a single parent and you want to know how you can properly raise your children without the help of your partner, then this book is for you. Here, you will be given tips on how to go about the situation of single parenthood. This book also hopes to answer questions regarding custody, housing, money, and a whole lot more.

Finally, this book aims to give hope to single parents who may be struggling to make ends meet and raise their children to become good individuals. The sole parent situation is difficult for both the parent and the children, but it is not impossible that you can win over the situation. If the custodial adult can remain strong despite the many disappointments and problems, the outlook for the children will turn excellent.

Thanks again for taking interest in this book, I hope you enjoy it!

Chapter 1: The Greatest Gift – Your Child

One of the most special experiences as a human being can have is to become a parent. To have and hold your own baby is priceless. There are simply no words to describe it. You have in your arms the greatest gift that this world can offer.

You will never forget your baby's first smile, first step, and first word. These moments will be forever in your heart. It's hard to fathom how such a small bundle can bring so much joy.

As your child grows older, there are many changes that are taking place. Sometimes, these changes make you feel that you are losing the bond that holds the two of you together. At first, it can be devastating. When you realize though that those changes is part of the intricate design of life, you become ready. You understand that part of growing up is change.

When your child reaches the teenage years, it is a whole new experience for the both of you. Some would describe raising their teenagers as difficult. Each experience is unique. Why not make yours wonderful?

The start of something big

Raising your teenager to become the mature, responsible and loving adults you want them to be is one of life's greatest achievements. There may be tests, there may be challenges, and there may even be tears along the way, but in the end, it will all be worth it. After all, your child deserves nothing but the best.

The teenage years are sometimes referred to as the drama years. A lot of emotions can take over during this time. Many parents actually dread this stage of their children's life. However, these years are something to look forward to. Why? These years are the start of something big - both for you and your teenager, that's why!

Are you ready to take this journey together with your teenager?

Getting to know your teenager

The teenage years are divided into three phases: the early teens cover the ages 13-14, mid teens - 15-17 and late teens 18-19. In each category, they exhibit different personalities and characteristics. This book will prepare you to manage each category with different approaches. The earlier you start knowing your teens, the better for you.

There are many theories that were developed to analyze this stage in life. One is that of Sigmund Freud – the

Psychosexual Theory. Freud called this stage the Genital Stage. It is here where adolescents have sexual experimentation. This information will come in handy to you as parents to prepare your teenagers for those questions they may have, or to have that "talk" objectively.

On the other hand, according to Eric Erickson's Psychosocial theory, this stage is the Identity versus Confusion phase. At this age, the teenagers are trying to discover who they are. They are searching for their true identities. During this stage, they try to establish independence and control. This is a very confusing time for them and rightly so. They are not considered children anymore, but they are also not considered adults yet. So what are they? It is as if they are in a limbo.

Erickson emphasized the need for teenagers to discover their true selves and identities so that they would develop the confidence and self-esteem, which will give them the strong direction in life so that they would be able to fit into society. Failure to do so, would lead to being confused, and insecure adults later on in life.

How do teenagers find their true identities?

This is the time when teenagers seek various ways to discover who they really are. They usually rely on other teenagers to help establish control, independence, and identity. They also rely on experimentation. What will work for them?What will not? Most of the time though, they rely on what is popular and trendy, in the hope that they will find out who they really are and who they are meant to be. As parents, you have a very special role in the development of these teenagers into responsible adults. Your responses to them are one of the factors that would determine how and who they would be in the future. The establishment of their independence and identities will depend on how well you manage the teenage years. You are already one step ahead. You have been there before.

Chapter 2: Nutrition

Ensure Proper Nutrition For Your Child

Proper nutrition for a child is essential for the mental and physical growth of the child. Whether you are breastfeeding your child or not, you should ensure that they always eat a balanced diet and by balanced diet, I mean that their meals should contain proteins, vitamins, carbohydrates and fats. Most newborns depend on breast milk as a source of all nutrients. If you do not plan on breastfeeding your newborn baby, you should seek a nutritionist's advice on how to feed your baby otherwise you risk depriving them of the necessary nutrients, which may result to complications later during their growth.

So why is nutrition so important? Here is why:

Proper nutrition strengthens a child's immune system. Lack of all the nutrients in a child's diet may lead to nutrient deficiency diseases, which you don't want.

Proper nutrition supports optimal growth. For a child to grow at a normal rate, he or she should be fed with a balanced diet. Most children appear smaller for their age because they may have lacked proper diets while growing up and hence had stunted growth. You should ensure that your child eats a balanced diet.

Child obesity prevention: Overweight children are of greater risk of developing major health issues such as high blood pressure, high cholesterol, cardiovascular diseases and even type 2 diabetes. Feeding your child well ensures that they minimize the risk of suffering from such lifestyle diseases.

So what happens if you don't observe the above?

Delay puberty

Increase risk of getting an eating disorder

Nutrient deficiency diseases

Poor academic performance

What not to feed your child

When a child starts eating real food (not just milk), many of us parents make terrible mistakes that end up messing our children in different ways in the name of loving them or giving them what we think is best for them. For instance, you might have grown to dislike certain foods that your parents gave you in your early years and decided that you cannot feed your child such kinds of food when in fact, these are the foods that ensured that you grew healthy and strong. So when you decide that you cannot feed your child such kinds of foods, you are definitely denying them what is good and offering stuff that you have subconsciously told yourself is better when in fact it is just empty in calories and nutrients. This is especially common with the modern parent who feels that they should give their children "trendy" or "cool" food and not the traditional whole meals. Well, you shouldn't make this terrible mistake. Failing to feed your child nutrient rich foods and instead give them highly processed foods (most of which are full of preservatives, added sugars and other additives) can end up causing different complications to your child. For instance, the more you feed the child with such processed foods, the higher the likelihood that the child might suffer from lifestyle diseases like diabetes, cardiovascular diseases, and the like.

You should also not:

Feed your child sugary things. Of course, buying your child an ice cream or a cake is not an offence but too much of everything is definitely not good. Limit your child's intake of sugary things especially because sugar contains many calories, which do not contain any essential nutrients. Additionally, too much sugar provides easy access to energy for the bad bacteria in the mouth, which might easily multiply and end up causing teeth problems like cavities or bad breath.

Feed your child on foods, which they are allergic to. Well, this might sound pretty obvious but please note that allergy doesn't have to be so extreme or life threatening. You need to be observant to note any allergic reactions that your child might be exhibiting. Also, ensure to inform everyone who interacts with the child about any allergies the child might be having. For instance, if you get a nanny, be sure to inform them about your child's allergy.

As a parent, sometimes it can be very confusing to figure out what it means to eat healthy, as far as your child is concerned. Fortunately, you don't need to have a degree in nutrition in order to bring up healthy kids. By following a few basic guidelines, you can encourage your kids to maintain a healthy weight and eat right. Here are a few rules to live by:

*Control the supply lines: You make the decision on which foods to purchase and when to serve it. While you kids may pester you for less nutritious foods, you should be in charge of deciding the kinds of foods to stock in your house. You can still get them that sweet snack occasionally to prevent them from feeling deprived.

*Let your kids choose from the foods provide: Kids need to make some contribution in the matter. Schedule regular snack and meal times, and let them choose from the options you offer. This may seem like too much freedom, but when there are only healthy foods on the table, your kids will be making a safe decision.

*Stop the clean plate routine: Your kids should stop eating when they feel they have had enough. Most parents were raised through the clean plate law, but this is not a very effective approach. Children are less likely to overeat when they notice and react to feelings of fullness.

*Start them young. Kids develop food preferences at an early age, so provide a variety. A child may need to be served a new food on different occasions before they learn to accept it. Offer a few bites, but do not force it on them.

*Rewrite their menu: Kids don't just want to eat cheese, macaroni, burgers, pizza and hot dogs. Allow your kids to try out new foods when eating out and they might surprise you with their eagerness to experiment.

*Watch drink calories: Sweetened drinks such as soda provide extra calories, and interfere with good nutrition. The best drinks for children are milk and water. They don't need juice much, but four to six ounces (100% pure) per day for preschoolers is enough.

*Regulate sweets: It's fine to offer occasional sweets, but don't let it be the main reason for taking dinner. Be neutral about your foods.

*Watch out for food rewards: There are better ways to say you love your kids than food. Using foods to show affection and reward your kids may lead them into using food to deal with stress and other emotions. Instead, offer praise, hugs, and attention.

*Kids copy what you do: Eat healthy and be a role model yourself. Try to set the best example as far as good eating habits are concerned. Avoid skipping meals, eat at the table, and choose nutritious snacks.

*Limit computer and TV time: This will help encourage activity and avoid mindless snacking. Studies have shown that children who cut down on television also tend to reduce their percentage body fat. Limiting computer and TV time will give them more time to do active things.

How much food do your kids need?

The daily calorie requirement for toddlers is 1,000 to 1,400 calories per day, depending on their size, age and activity level. Here are some guidelines for the average two and three year old.

Chapter 3: Developing Moral Values And conscious Parenting

In order to obtain better comprehension about Conscious Parenting, here are ways on how to develop moral values and Conscious Parenting –

1. Being insightful

The most crucial thing that is essentially required to adopt the method of conscious parenting is being insightful. With an insightful mind, the parents can easily understand the characteristic inclination of their child and effortlessly mold their moral values accordingly.

2. Re-evaluation of decisions

It is also essential for the guardians to possess a flexible approach in terms of making decisions related to their children to become a successful conscious parent. Being rigid on decisions can cause adverse effects on the life of the children.

3. Concentrating onwiderinterpretation

The major focus of a conscious parent must be on the long term benefit and betterment of the child. They generally keep wider perspectives of interpreting what their child says and does on a regular basis for their complete personality development.

4. Priority to relationship

For a conscious parent the top most priority is their relation with the child. They generally keep everything secondary when their relationship is at risk.

5. Acting wisely

Conscious parents are also required to be thoughtful while acting as it reflects their positive and appropriate reactions towards the children.

6. Ensuring mutual respect

The significant concern of Conscious Parenting is on the concept of mutual respect. It is just equivalent to the process of give and take. It is not the children only who have to give respect to their parents. The parents are also essentially required to pay certain amount of respect to their children.

7. Speak less and inquire more

Another crucial principle of conscious parenting involves the parents to speak minimum and inquire more. They must constantly inquire about the preferences, choices and requirements of their children as it helps in understanding their psyche in a better way.

8. Being attentive towardschild's age

The conscious parents are very much attentive towards the growing age of their children. They efficiently deal with their children by strictly according to their age. The thoughtful capability of kids gradually grows with their age and thus the parents are required to act accordingly for their effective development.

9. Avoidingunnecessary negations

Some parents have this tendency to say 'NO' to their kids every time they raise any demand without understanding its relevance. However, a conscious parent generally avoids saying unnecessary "NO" to his child. They generally negate on some strong and credible reasons.

10. Nurturingfaith

Trust and faith also plays a crucial role in the method of Conscious Parenting. A conscious parent also cultivates trust and faith with his child that consequently results in the conformity and obedience of their kids. The development of mutual trust reflects confidence and acceptancein the relationship.

Significant Ways of Becoming a Conscious Parent

Becoming a conscious parent requires huge preparation of the mind as well as the heart to deal with any kind of situations. In order to become an efficient conscious parent, we provide some crucial traits that are essentially required in a conscious parent. With the development of these traits, the relationship of both parents and kids will become strong along with positive approaches of parenting.

Developing poignantrelations

The most essential goal of child rearing is to construct a poignant relation among the parents and the child. The very basic foundation of children's growth is based on the truthful and firm bond of emotions between both of them. In order to produce an outstanding passionate bond, the parents are required to be receptive towards their child's psychological, emotional as well as materialistic requirements.

Offering support and protection

Another significant trait which is essentially required to become a conscious parent is to offer a secure environment to the children along with being supportive. It is very essential to develop the thought of being safe and secure in the company of their parents.

Sympathizing

An effective sympathizing nature of the parents is also essentially required to become a conscious parent. It basically involves understanding the ideas and feelings of the children by keeping yourself in their shoes. It is the most influential and reliable way of becoming a successful cognizant parent.

Getting involved in conscious parenting

It requires huge amount of practice as well as attention to understand parenting in a better way. An ultimate experience can be gathered by significantly understanding the actions, reaction and behavior of the child. There are certain possibilities of occurrence of mistakes on parent's part which is completely normal. These mistakes provide a life time lesson for the parents to learn which possess the capability to produce highly effective and positive results.

Fosteringchild's prospective

It is also essential for the parents to understand the inherent skills and talents present in their children and help them in fostering them effectively. Identification of child's interest and his potential skills prove to be of significant utility for the parents to establish an effective bond of togetherness with their children. Conscious parents are required to encourage and support the skills present in their children. They do not force their aspirations on their kids rather they allow them to do the things of their interest.

Maintain own happiness and fitness

The very primary step for a happy and successful parenting is to maintain your own happiness and fitness. It is a natural as well as psychological fact that most of the children are inspired from their parents. If the parents take effective care of themselves, the children will automatically learn the excellent quality of taking care of themselves.

Being comprehensive and participating

Contradict the traditional method of creating distinctions with your children. It increases the significant gap between a parent and child relationship. The conscious parenting desires effective involvement and participation of parents as well as children in the activities of both the segments. The parents should involve themselves in the playful activities of the kids whereas the children should show active participation in the interesting activities of parents. The more time they spend together, the more strong and effective relation can be established.

Being pleased with your child

One of the most significant things that were found deficient in the conventional method of parenting was lack of appreciation for the kids by the parents. However, for conscious parenting, it is very essential to treat your child and appreciate his talent as well as good deeds. Not only this, it also involves considerationof the efforts laid by them.

Chapter 4: Kids And Gadgets

Recently while visiting a colleague's home, I was amazed at how bored her two year old was with sitting among the adults and not interested at all in her coloring book. The next thing I noticed is she walked down from her parent's room upstairs and had her mother's iPad with her. She knew how to operate it, she knew where her mother kept it and she knew which icon to click so that she could entertain herself by watching cartoons on it. It is unbelievable as to how a kid these days knows how to use a gadget as well as how to use their feeding bottle.

Action figures, building blocks etc. are no longer of any interest to children when visiting the toy store. Research conducted by the specialists at the Michael Cohen group in a recent study have revealed that standard toys now available across the play stores in the country have touch screens which have taken over all other toys as a medium of delightfor kids. Several parents who participated in the survey have reported that their children which accounts for sixty percent of the survey have their own portable screen device and play on it often, while forty percent who don't own their own device but use their parents or older sibling's devices play more than often. The children in this survey are all below the age of 12 years. Shocking isn't it? The research also revealed that most children by age 4 stopped playing outdoors and were happier sitting indoors with their portable screen device.

Physical play or Playing outdoors as we refer to it has enormous advantages from mental to physical to emotional. Before you even consider giving in to your child's tantrum just so he shuts up, think again. Parents prefer gadgets as a way to pacify their wailing child rather than deal with their own child to understand what is wrong. However, later on it does turn into an alarming sight especially with gadgets getting more affordable by the day. Modern gadgets have long-term effects on a child's brain and also impact their overall development. Several experts are advising families to reduce the exposure their children especially toddlers have to electronic gadgets. Below are some of the reasons why you as a super mom need to keep gadgets away from your child.

Brain Development

Even before your child can begin talking and utter his/her first word, their brain is growing in size i.e. you child learns a lot and observes much more than you and me assume before they can even turn five years old and the learning continues till they are adults. The University of Washington has released a report which states that electronic gadgets are not essential in development of a child. In fact, they recommend to most parents to engage in conversations and read to their child to ensure development. As a Supermom in the internet age, you need to ensure that you are spending one on one time with your child and not allowing your child to take that time away from you only to spend it in front of a gadget. Research has proven that over exposure to any kind of electronic gadget can lead to negative effect on the functioning of the brain, attention deficiency, impaired learning and cognitive delays.

Delayed Language Skills

As per the Academy of Pediatrics in America, educational TV is nothing but a sham. While presumptions are made that screen time can be educational the Academy states that toddlers under the age of four do not have the skills to understand what is going on in the program. Educational TV interferes with 'bonding time' which the parent and child need to share, but lack of bonding time results in delayed language skills. So the next time you even consider getting your child or your niece or any kid below the age of five years an electronic gadget and consider it to be useful or for educational purposes, think again. Not only will you be wasting some good money which can be invested in your child elsewhere, it will also hamper his/her development. Handing over a gadget to any child before he can even walk and talk is a disaster in the making.

Obesity

Parents who rely on gadgets and the television to keep their child entertained all the time have no clue how much damage they are doing to their child. Children make it a habit to stay indoors with their gadgets or lazing around on the couch in front of their screens rather than go outside and play. Fewer playtimes leads to childhood obesity. Two in every five children in the country are obese, and unless parents take constructive action to help the child in reducing his/her weight, they are bound to grow up into adults suffering from various complications such as heart disease, diabetes just to name a few. Parents, especially a mother must encourage her child to play more. Not only does a child get fit at a playground, he also learns to develop relationships with the other children which will help him to learn to socialize at an early age. Encouraging kids into more physical activity or even exposure to physical activity works like magic instead of inculcating technology in their early years. Physical activity helps promote a healthier lifestyle for the children as they grow. Restriction in movement also leads to delayed development of the bones in a child. The benefits of playing outdoors are not just limited to building relationships and staying physically fit, a small amount of time playing, even if it means just 20 – 30 minutes changes the way the brain functions in a child. Exercise will also help in tiring out your child which means less tantrums and peaceful sleep! So encouraging your child to go out and play isn't just beneficial for the child but for you as well!

Less Sleep-Time

Once a child is handed over any gadgets, it will lead to addiction unless it is used in controlled measure. However, controlling a child's addiction to gadgets is difficult with most parents tough working hours. This results in the child missing out on essential rest time. The gadget becomes an addictive sleeping pill for the child. The glow of the laptop screen and mobile phones deprive the children of a good night's sleep. Parents who do not supervise their children's gadget use and allow them to use gadgets in their bedrooms have stated that they do wake up to cranky and irritable children due to less sleep time. If you suddenly stop your child from using a gadget he is used to having with him in bed, he could get aggressive and wake up extremely grumpy. It gets worse if you have a child who goes to school. Sleep-deprived children are known to have a bad report card in school along with learning issues. Researchers have found that most students living in developing countries with limited access to gadgets have a better report card with good grades in Math and Reading unlike their counterparts in the U.S and other developed economies where children are known to be overexposed to electronic gadgets.

No Learning Exposure

Gadgets kill the development and learning exposure of a child. Instead of learning how a plant grows, or running around learning to play a sport, rolling in dirt, kids with gadgets prefer staying home staring at their screens and learning the ways of the world. That does not benefit them in any way and only causes more harm. If a child is unable to feel a plant, or injure himself while playing, he will never be able to understand how the world functions without experiencing it. Without any exposure, a child can't learn anything, can he? Overprotective parents who feel their child is better off at home, secure from the rest of the world are sadly mistaken. Toddlers can learn a lot from interaction and experiencing.

Reduced interaction due to children spending more time with technology and less time with people disrupts the communication development process of a child. When surrounded by family, a toddler might be unable to improve his communication but his interaction with his family improves and he is able to identify and feel safe and comfortable around others as well. Children who are left exposed to television or gadgets inherit their talking skills from the television but fail when they try to communicate or socialize with other people.

Aggression in Children

The National Institute of Health in a study conducted by them have found that dependence of kids on gadgets and other electronic items result in a child not being able to inherit good family values, behavior and over all general well-being.

Games on the internet contain acts of violence, sex, which can be critical to the upbringing of a child. Games containing such aggressive behavior are known to create aggression in a child if he is accustomed to playing such games or watching such videos at a young age. As a child's brain develops over time, he will want to try out something he has seen before, but never done it himself. Children who are addicted to their gadgets and video games are more likely the ones who will disobey and create their own rules. So instead of depending on the gadgets to keep your child calm opt for games and toys which will keep your child occupied long enough to tire him out.

As a modern Mom, if we continue to feed the whims and fancies of our children, we are allowing their aggression to grow. Parents need to understand that exposing a child to the rest of the world is in the best of their interest, instead of leaving them at home with their gadgets. Instead of getting a child addicted to electronic gadgets and other fancy technologies, we as parents must ensure that our children are exposed to activities which help promote proper emotional, physical and mental development.

If you have just introduced your child to a new gadget, moderate its use by your child. Instead introduce your child to new habits such as playing outdoor games with children his age, reading informative books thereby inculcating good reading habits and doing your own research on educational toys for his development.

Damaged Eyesight

Excessive exposure of the eyes to the phone or computer screens leads to the eyes getting strained. Good eyesight depends on staring at things at different distances. Children of any age group who are addicted to their phones or computer screens are the ones who are more likely to have damaged eyesight than other children.

While it is not recommended to not allow a child at all to use a computer, moderation should be maintained by the parents if they allow their child to find information on a computer. Over exposed eyes will begin to hurt the child's vision and will hinder the child's vision. One in five kids these days has vision problems because of being glued to the television or the computer non-stop. They won't eat without watching television. They won't sleep without watching their favorite show at night. This needs to stop, and as a modern Supermom, you need to know where to pull the plug, quite literally.

Working on screens can weaken vision in kids if the screen is viewed closely, since it forces the eye's lens to adjust to shorter distances. Double vision or blurred vision, eyes drying up, eye fatigue and eyes turning red are just some of the issues kids complain about to their parents these days. Blue light or the light from the phone and computer screen is more harmful to kids since their pupils are larger and have clearer lenses which allow more of the blue light to reach the retina. Less time spent using devices and more time spent outdoors can help as a solution to less eye trouble.

Gadget Tantrums

A new word has been coined quite recently for children who throw a tantrum when their electronic gadgets are taken away from them. As a punishment, if you or anyone (including any authorized person at your child's school) confiscates the electronic gadget belonging to the child, there will be an "ipaddy" moment. Since your child would be addicted and attached to the gadget, they are going to throw quite a nasty tantrum, anything which will let them have their gadget back. If you don't want to be a mother who is called to school in the middle of a busy work day because your child has had an "ipaddy" situation, you need to re-look and assess the amount of time you allow your child to spend with any electronic gadget in your house.

Technology will only grow and there is no stopping it. As a parent, we must learn how to get our children to adapt to life without the use of a fancy electronic device. If however, the damage has already been done, and your child suffers several ipaddy moments, you need to sit your child down and explain the consequences, i.e. the advantages along with the disadvantages. When you supervise your child's gadget addiction habits, the device can help in development at the right age, but introducing a gadget or device at an early age and excessive use of it can lead to a significant delay in a child's learning capabilities as well as affecting his health and general disposition.

While the above points discussed in brief are not meant to scare you, they will help you in controlling your children's gadget addiction. Several research studies have shown that children whose gadget or electronic device habits are not monitored end up spending approximately seven to eight hours staring at their device screen. No wonder then, our country ranks high in the number of obese children and low grades on average. Traditional play grounds have been found to make children more sociable by enhancing their social skills as well as calmer in their general disposition.

In the internet age, kids do not need any hassles of unpacking a board game. Who wants to clean up once playtime is over? No kid wants to twist a Play-Doh and model it on something when the same can be done on any electronic device like an iPad. Instant gratification is what kids these days are on the lookout for. Your child is no longer a sweet little walking talking toddler, in today's world, children are now beginning to behave like little adults, and if we don't keep a lookout, we are going to be depriving them of their childhood and its innocence.

Chapter 5: Effective Positive Parenting Tips

Positive parenting helps you make the best decisions for your child. There is no such thing as an ideal parent who is a totally confident parent all the time, but you can learn specific tips to help guide your children with more confidence toward a better life in the future. If positive parenting techniques are not applied, then chances are the child will automatically be inclined to focus on the negative side of life.

Parenting strategies work when the child is in the process of growing, and the brain is developing. A child learns by observing first and then receiving an explanation verbally, so it is always better to portray positive parenting in your daily actions. In other words, live the life you want your children to have one day and they will be much more likely to have a healthy and well-balanced childhood because of it.

Top 10 Tips for Positive Parenting

1. Be the Model

Children need guidance and a figure they can look up to and admire. Be that person in your child's life by giving them a clear example to follow. For example, if you ask your child to throw their trash in the trash bin, then you have to do the same. Show them through action and they will learn. Children look up to their parents and imitate their actions more than anyone else. They also watch their parents closely, even when the parent may not be aware, so be vigilant and conscious of your actions at all times. You have to be the person you want your child to be. If you show them a positive attitude, they will learn from it and do the same.

2. Be Loving

Know that love is something which can never spoil a child. Show your love through hugs, kisses, spending time together, talking about mutually exciting topics, listening to the music he/she likes and much more. Love does not have to be materialistic, just meaningful – anything which can create memories for a lifetime. Showing love to a child can help them develop a sense of calm and contentment. It introduces them to the emotional side of nature which brings resilience and creates a close relationship with the parent.

3. Staying Positive

Try to not influence your child with your own negativity, even if you are hit with a challenge that brings out negative emotions. Rather than expressing negativity, try to think of ways to approach the situation with a positive attitude. Share your positive personality with your child so their brain learns to have positive thoughts no matter what the circumstance may be. Share positive experiences with them so they can have hope and goodwill.

4. Be There for the Child

Always be available for the child no matter what the problem is. Do not underestimate their ability to handle the situation on their own, but at the same time always be the safety spot for them. Support your child when they need you because it develops trust and closeness. Be responsive to a child because it directly affects their emotional development, and the outcomes of this approach are always positive.

5. Always Communicate

Make sure you keep small conversations on the go every day and recognize the importance of communication with your child. Do not miss a day without talking to them. Always listen to your child and talk to him/her carefully with understanding and respect for his/her perspective. Ask about any event which happened and listen to how he/she dealt with it. You do not have to impose your opinion but just quietly listen to their view and acknowledge what they share. Keep an open dialogue, so he/she can talk about anything without hesitation or fear. Great communication between a parent and child makes the child more cooperative and friendly as they grow up.

6. Change Your Parenting Style

Do not follow the same route your parents took with you to deal with your child. While your parents may have been great, there is always room for improvement and what worked for you may not be as effective with your own child. Observe positive parenting techniques and take notes on how you can do even better as a parent. Change your behavior positively and you are bound to see a good result come of it gradually, if not immediately.

7.Maintain Your Well-Being

To implement positive parenting solutions, it is necessary that you have things sorted out on your end. You need to pay attention to your relationship with your spouse and the things that you manage like your house and finances so that your brain is calm. Once you are calm and everything is fine on your end, then you are in a better position to raise a child to the best of your ability. If the relationship with your spouse is weak, then it will surely hurt the child directly or unintentionally. Take care of yourself in the best way you can, so you are at peace mentally and physically and can give your very best self to parenting.

8. Do Not Spank Your Child

Never spank your child even if you are playing with him/her. Spanking can become a regular habit for the parents to punish the child to make him/her understand they are misbehaving. It undoubtedly does not leave a good impression on the child though, so do not think you are controlling the child's thoughts in any way. The method of spanking does nothing but teach a child to act up even more in defiance. It explains to the child what the worst consequence of his or her actions looks like and prepares them next time to do the same thing and hide from you to avoid getting a spanking, which ultimately has not taught them anything. So, it is better to hold them or stop them verbally and calmly explain why you are preventing them from the action or behavior.

By hitting your child, you teach him/her that you can sort out any issue through violence. The child learns that instead of sorting out disputes calmly, they can bully people with physical violence and get their way.

9. Keep a Goal in Mind

How do you want your child to be when he/she grows up? Every parent has a dream that their child will possess a particular kind of behavior which the parent appreciates. Keep that goal in mind while you are raising your child. If you want your child to be positive, kind, helpful, and empathic, then show them how to be those things so they can follow by example. It's easy to lose sight of what you want for your child in the midst of daily challenges. That's why it is so important to take a step back from time to time, look at the bigger picture, and re-adjust your approach with your long-term goal for your child in mind.

10. Never Stop Learning

If you get angry at your child unreasonably then do some research online or at your local library to find out how you can overcome such behavior. If you struggle with discipline, write down your thoughts and seek advice on the subject to find a better approach you are comfortable with You have to spend time thinking about how to raise your child, and positive parenting can champion the best parent in you. The key here is never to stop learning and growing as a parent.

Chapter 6: What Makes Parenting Seem Problematic?

In order to know why parenting is becoming a nuisance, there some things you might be doing wrong. Take a look;

· **Not following routine-** if you want to handle preschoolers, consistency is the key. It does not make sense to allow your baby do something but the next time you are against it. The kid will get confused. She will not understand why.

For instance, yesterday you allowed her to watch television the whole day but today you want her to watch for only three hours. She might even throw tantrums because she will not understand why it is not like the previous day.

You see, if she knows she is only supposed to watch television for a given period of time, she is likely to follow it apart from rare occasions.

Let consistency prevail, be it discipline, mealtime habits or sleeping routines.

· **Concentrating too much on the negative** many parents have a tendency of concentrating on what they do not want their children to do. If you always find yourself saying phrases like "don't hit your friend", "don't throw stones", "don't do this or that", maybe that is where your problem is.

It is okay to say that but it also good to recognize and reward good habits. Rewards to positive behavior can be like clapping for them, giving them a big hug, kissing them, praising them and encouraging them to do good all the time.

These things may seem petty but they really work for preschoolers.

· **Failure to read warning signs** if your child starts to throw tantrums, it is important to understand why she is reacting that way. Many times parents start calming the child down and before they know it, the child is out of control. Mostly the signs are for hunger, boredom or fatigue. Sometimes she may be unwell.

I advise parents not to take their children out in public unless they have been well fed and have had enough rest and sleep. To be safe, carry with you their favorite snack.

· **Parents encourage whining without even knowing** so now you are busy trying to finish some work you carried from work. Say like balancing account books of record. Your daughter comes to you and says that she wants ice cream. You say no because it is could out there. She starts crying and throwing tantrums. Because you are busy you give in and allow her to have the ice cream. With time she will learn which button to push whenever she needs anything.

If you ignore her sulking and whining she will finally know that that does not work.

- **Giving your child too many responsibilities** if you want your child to attend music classes, drama classes and other activities after school then that is too much for her to handle. Her brain is still young and she needs time to calm down and release all her tension. School alone is already exhausting for her.

Allow her to engage in her own free play after school.

- **Not playing with children** it is very true that your child is capable of playing alone. However, that does not mean that you should not take time playing with them.

You might be busy but make sure to allocate time to play with your preschooler. This way she is able to open up to you. The bond gets stronger and you are more likely to know if something is bothering her.

- **Overreacting to lies** at this age, your child knows what getting in trouble really means and wants to escape the consequences. He will therefore try to experiment with a lie. Make sure you don't yell or beat them up. Calmly ask them to tell the truth and tell them that you understand.

Try to make them understand that you know they feel bad about what they did but they should know that lying is not good.

Chapter 7: Parents Need To Agree On Parenting Methods

One of the most important things that parents need do while planning a blended family, is to sit down and discuss their parenting methods very openly and honestly with each other. This is so valuable for ANY people who want to co-parent a child or children together. Nothing can cause a broken marriage faster than two people who do not agree on how to parent their children.

When bringing a new parent into a situation, whether there are other kids or not, it is of major importance that the parents are all on the same page. There is no need to change all of the rules with a new parent. Children need stability.

Parents should make all necessary adjustments to their parenting styles so that they are supporting each other.Children learn very quickly which parent cannot be consistent, and they will play one parent against the other one.Be a team and earn your children's respect together; and insist on that respect from the kids.And that respect refers to not only the parents, but also for each other (all of the family members).

There are so many things to think about when you look at parenting styles.First there is discipline.Agree on how you want to discipline your children.Be fair and consistent.There are many different styles of discipline.You both need to discuss them in depth.If one parent is against corporal punishment, this must be respected by both parties.Most parents are moving away from spanking these days, but not agreeing on this one is a reason to NOT bring this relationship to a marriage. One parent cannot be a spanker when the other parent is not.

Think about it, how is the parent who hates spanking going to feel when he/she sees the other parent spanking his/her child?What will the other children think when they see their punishment is so different from their step siblings?This sends such mixed messages; and will ultimately bring an end to the family structure, as well as the marriage.

When the parents can agree on the punishment methods, they then need to discuss rewards and consequences.Again, these must be consistent and fair to all of the children in the blended family.They will not be responsive to your rules if they are not fair, or if you do not enforce them.Some people like to involve their children in helping to set the rules for the family.

This is where the parents will start the family rules with some "Non-negotiables." These are absolute rules that are set in stone. They will be rules like always respecting each other and each other's property; no hitting or cursing; no friends in the house when parents are not at home, etc.

Let the kids help to decide on their chores and responsibilities around the house. When they help to make the decisions, they will make them their own, and they will not only respect their own rules, but they will help to encourage their siblings to do the same, holding each other responsible.

Agree on bedtimes for the children, enforce them, and be consistent. Parents should agree on and enforce homework rules as well. The transition is much smoother if the parents are a united team.

Chapter 8: How You Shape Your Baby's Brain

In the previous chapter, we talked about how emotional regulation works. In times of challenge or fear, the stress response kicks in, giving us the energy and drive to get out of trouble. In times of safety, the calm and connection circuit takes over, allowing for rest and rejuvenation.

That description applies to a healthy, fully mature brain. But this brain development, including the PFC's ability to inhibit impulses and override the amygdala's emotional hair-trigger, won't be fully complete until your child is almost 23 years old. At newborn to two years old, your child's brain is at the very beginning of the developmental journey. At this stage, you act as the co-pilot for your baby's amygdala.

This is called **co-regulation** and it's a profound and amazing thing. But it's very simple. **Regulation** is our ability to respond appropriately to stress and connection without going to extremes. We need to be able to tolerate a certain amount of stress in order to respond to the demands of daily life — as well as to some of the more extreme demands, such as jumping out of the way of a car.

To understand regulation, think of the thermostat in a house. When it's working right, it keeps the house at a nice, steady 70 degrees. When a cold wind blows, the thermostat tells the furnace to put out some heat. When the sun beats down, the thermostat tells the furnace to turn itself off.

In this analogy, stress is that cold wind, prompting us to amp up a bit to deal with things. The opportunity to relax or connect is the warm sun, soothing the HPA axis and revving up the calm and connection system.

But your thermostat can go on the blink. It may turn the furnace on when it gets cold, but not signal it to turn off when the house has warmed up enough. Or, it may let the house get really chilly before it turns on the furnace. In our analogy, your brain may not be able to turn off the furnace of emotion in response to stress. Or, it may not be able to rouse your emotions to react. Both are forms of dysregulation. Emotional dysregulation is the inability to control your mood.

Your most important job as a parent of a newborn to three-year-old is to train your child's emotional thermostat to keep on an even keel, that is, to regulate the body/mind/emotions.

Now, think about a house where the windows are old and leaky. There's no insulation, and drafts rush in under the front door. The thermostat may work okay, but it has to constantly adjust the furnace in an attempt to keep the temperature somewhat even. If the house is well-insulated, on the other hand, it's easy to maintain comfort. A parent's love and care in the first three years of life acts as emotional insulation, giving a child a secure base from which to meet the challenges and disappointments of life. Without this emotional insulation, a child may over-react to little things like being corrected by a teacher or being denied a cookie.

In the period between newborn and three, a parent co-regulates with the child. Co-regulation is more than modeling behavior or guiding a child's interactions with you. In co-regulation, your body and your child's actually synch up, communicating directly below the level of consciousness.

Because this is a deep body/mind communication, you cannot help your child learn to regulate if you are not able to regulate yourself. In fact, much of the work of parenting is work on yourself.

If your bodymind is not well-regulated, you give mixed messages to your child when she becomes **dysregulated**. For example, there comes a time in every parent's life when the child says, "You don't love me." The response is, "Of course, I love you. I'm your mother (or father)." While you may think your child is saying this to manipulate you, he may be expressing his true experience of you in that moment. While your core feeling may be a deep love for the child, in that moment, your emotional expression may be anger or fear. Your child is giving you a clear and direct message that he needs something different from you. He needs you to respond from a place of calm and connection.

Co-regulation is about more than suppressing fear; maybe even more important is increasing your child's capacity for joy and love. Every experience of pleasure and security encourages her brain to release oxytocin. This oxytocin release increases the number and sensitivity of oxytocin receptors in the social part of the brain. Practicing connection strengthens the brain's circuits for love and connection.

Emotional weather

Edward Tronick, an associate professor of pediatrics and psychiatry at Children's Hospital Boston, says that, very early, babies develop a predominant mood. That is, one baby becomes more likely to be content while another one develops the habit of being anxious. While every baby is capable of a wide range of emotions and moods, the tendency to develop a habitual mood is shaped both by her internal state and her parents' emotional input.

According to Tronick's theory, your baby normally cycles through different states in which she's more or less receptive to being in a certain mood. You can encourage that mood or not.

For example, in some parts of the cycle, she's more receptive to positive emotions. If you play with her while she's in this part of the cycle, she'll react with joy and fall into a positive mood. After that first bit of play, it will take even less to make her smile and laugh.

On the other hand, if she's not in the part of the cycle when she's receptive to joy, she may not respond to your tickles and giggles.

She will also naturally be more susceptible to negative emotions at different times. When she's in a cranky mood, it doesn't take much to get her crying, while it's harder to please her.

Tronick thinks that the intensity of the emotion you show to your baby combined with how long you interact that way influences how deep into that mood the baby will sink and how long it will last.

Quite simply, a happy mother will be more likely to raise a happy baby, while a grouchy mom can increase the susceptibility to bad moods. This is not to say that your baby should never be fussy and always happy. Remember that it's natural for her to cycle through these moods.

You're acting as a co-regulator of your baby's natural states. Your actions influence the baby's release of cortisol or oxytocin, and your baby's behavior influences your own state. As you use Oxytocin Parenting to teach your baby to regulate, you are lovingly encouraging her to feel at home in a state of calm and connection with you.

Parenting Your Child's Brain

As the grown-up and the parent, you have so much responsibility for your child's physical and emotional development. This can make it easy to forget that, as much as your relationship with your child in the first two years of life guides her development, the relationship changes you, as well.

This is a key concept of oxytocin parenting and the basis of our approach at the Post Institute. As a unique individual, you bring the sum of your emotional experience and learning to the relationship with your newborn. As you enter into and maintain this relationship, each of you responds to the other.

Alan Fogel, a professor of developmental psychology at the University of Utah, uses dynamic systems theory to explain nonverbal, unconscious interaction. According to dynamic systems theory, nothing in nature is isolated and nothing remains the same — including human relationships. Your own emotions are part of the greater system that's your relationship with your family, friends, coworkers, your religion or spiritual beliefs, even your nation.

When you look at the way patterns form in nature, according to Fogel, it's clear that big differences may begin with very tiny differences. These little differences, for example, how long it takes for a mother to respond to her baby's cries, reinforce certain patterns while weakening others. Over time, one little thing can turn into a very strong predilection that lasts our whole lives.

In Relationships that Support Human Development, Fogel writes, "All interpersonal relationships tend to evolve or grow into a number of recognizable patterns, some of which lead people into a fuller and more creative relationship with the self and others of which lead to a more constrained and apparently painful relationship with the self and others."

Your ability to calm your child's fear, and to teach her to self-soothe, depends on your ability to do this for yourself. In the newborn to two stage, when you react with fear to a situation, your child will mirror your fear. Only when you can react to events and be present in the relationship with love will she be able to learn the oxytocin response.

What about Discipline?

In Oxytocin Parenting, everything you do is oriented toward relationship: triggering the oxytocin response. Being a loving, responsive and regulated parent does not mean that you're never upset. It does not mean that you don't set limits. It does not mean that you don't discipline. But this approach puts a different spin on the idea of discipline.

The core of who we are is nonverbal and is unconscious. Therefore, it's not what you say or do but how you feel when you're saying and doing it. You shouldn't "act nice" when you don't feel nice, nor should you feel that you have to walk on eggshells. If you're walking on eggshells, you're already stressed out.

Dad used to say, "I'm giving you this whipping because I love you and want you to learn." Or, "I'm sending you to your room without dinner because you have to learn manners and respect. If I didn't love you, I wouldn't care." These are not examples of Oxytocin Parenting.

We have been taught that love includes spanking, yelling, control, force, power, punishment, and much more, but these actions are fear disguised as love. The reason we struggle with love and to be "in love" so much is that we seldom get to experience true love. Love is understanding, flexibility, acceptance, tolerance, patience, and faithfulness. In love, there is joy and pain, worry and concern, but those states don't last when we dwell in love. Instead, they are fleeting.

You certainly will get upset and even angry with your kids. You can and should honor your feelings, understanding that some behavior has triggered your own fear. When you can do this, you can express your anger without shaming or blaming your child. As you do that, you'll find yourself calming down and moving back into regulation, while staying in relationship with the child.

If you lose it and do say something hurtful, you simply go back and apologize and repair the relationship. Your ability to repair the relationship shows your child that human beings can get angry or upset, but this doesn't mean that they won't love you anymore. This is not about perfect parenting; it's about taking responsibility and staying present in the relationship.

When your children see that you set limits based on what's best for her and not as punishment, she learns the value of limits. And, when you stay connected as you discipline, she gains a deeper experience of relationship.

Oxytocin Parenting means taking care of yourself, finding things that will bring you more oxytocin, reducing your own stress. Then, acting from a place of calm and love, you are able to take away your child's stress and fear.

Will My Kids Be Too Soft?

A big fear parents have is that if they are "too nice" to their kids, they will be shocked when they get out into the "real world." Some parents think they need to toughen up their children in by making them undergo stressful experiences at home. They want their kids to build up a hard emotional shell, so that they won't buckle under the inevitable hardships of adult life.

Consider this theory in light of a traveler undertaking a difficult journey through a desert. To prepare, should she drink as little water as possible? Would this keep her from being thirsty?

Of course not. Depriving herself of water would give her less endurance and less chance of completing the journey.

It's the same with love and joy. When you parent softly, you're giving your child a reservoir of love that she can draw on in times of loneliness and pain. She will be more resilient, more able to handle stress.

And she will also be better equipped to find and accept emotional support from other people.

When she inevitably encounters the anger and craziness of this society, she'll compare it to the love and connection she experienced in her family. She'll know that there's a better way to live, and she won't stop until she finds others who can give her the same kind of love and connection that she got from you.

Chapter 9: Working On Yourself To Become A Better Parent

It is important to recognize that we are all human, parents and kids alike. We all make mistakes. We all have things that trigger us to want to strangle one another. It is also vital to realize that slipups will happen while raising your kids on an almost daily basis.

A prime example of this is asking your child nicely to clean up their room. The first time, they are bound to ignore your request. This causes you to be a touch more demanding, in which they finally begin to pick up their toys. Many parents usually lean towards threatening, begging, and even negotiating. Yet, nothing works and your child ends up becoming defiant. You lose it and may yell at them, probably something similar to, "You are driving me nuts! Just do what I tell you to do!"

Learning to Let Go of the Past

We all have triggers that make us act out as adults in ways we may be ashamed of. While there are many articles that discuss how to become less stressed as a parent and all that jazz, I have found that it is more important to take a peak into the past in order to pinpoint why certain things trigger us to act out. Think about the relationship between you and your parents growing up, because it can be a heavy influence as to why you act the way you do with your children. Incidents that occurred during our own childhood can stir things up within us emotionally when similar situations happen with our own kids. When we lose control, it usually stems from an underlying past issue that we experienced growing up ourselves.

As you can imagine, this negativity can easily be passed down from generation to generation because we do not realize we continuously feed our own children with the same actions that made us who we are today. It is a domino effect that can be stopped if only parents took the time to recognize this simple fact. When we overcompensate for ways we were hurt previously in our lives, we project this right into our own kids, who then become a reflection of who we are. We forget that children are their own entities, which causes us to act in ways that are not aligned with what they need.

To counteract the past to better the future of our lives and the lives of our mini-me's, it is crucial to ask yourself how you might be acting like your parents did back in the day. Be honest with yourself. I suggest writing things down as you ponder about your childhood. Look into both words and actions. We tend to say things without much thought, such as "Listen to me because I am the boss" or "Because I said so." Consciously think about things you say or want to say, because oftentimes they stem directly from what our parents told us growing up. Despite how much you dislike or like your parents, we tend to behave in similar nature to our parent's personalities without realizing that we are.

As humans, we naturally internalize things that once hurt us. These attitudes are then converted into our point of view, which is then applied to our lives as we raise our own kids. Because your children are your creations, negative ways we view ourselves can easily be projected onto them without much thought. This is why the "domino effect of parenting" I mentioned earlier creates such a major impact. This is why it is so important to take the time to make sense of our own personal story. It is in this we are better able to recognize negative patterns in our behavior that can later be imprinted on our own kids.

The happier we are within ourselves, the more content and independent our kids will be able to become. It is vital to look within yourself and work on your own personal life when it seems that things are not going quite as well as they could be in your household. Being able to differentiate our own traits from our childhood can help create a much better growing up experience for your children, thus, ending the cycle of chaos that has inevitably been in your family for possibly generations.

Commitments to Becoming the Best Parent You Can Be

If you are a parent like me, you know that parenting is the biggest and hardest job you will ever do. Many of us go to bed at night thinking we never do a good enough job. We promise ourselves to make it a point to be more patient with our kids the next day, but this resolution never quite works. You cannot pour from an empty pot, meaning you have to give to yourself in order to successfully give to others in positive ways. If you cannot manage your own thoughts, feelings, and emotions, how can you expect your kids to do the same? Below are some commitments you should make to yourself to ensure that your kids have the best role model they can possibly have!

Commit to Caring for Yourself

Carrying out ways that allow you to stay centered will help you to be encouraging, patient, kind, and happy. This is the kind of parent that your kid deserves! Make it a priority to self-nurture in whatever ways you see fit.

Go to bed earlier to ensure adequate rest.

Eat healthy to balance moods.

Stop negative self-talk and encourage positivity.

Slow down and enjoy life. Make sure you do something for you on occasion.

Commit to Truly Loving Your Partner

Child development has many various points of views across the board, but there is one thing that is for certain: children that truly feel loved and cherished thrive. This means that the entire family should feel the love and compassion that all families should instill. Take time to really attend to your partner's needs when you can, and vice versa. A loving relationship between you and your partner shows your kids how to be a loving person later down the road.

Commit to Being Connected

Take even the smallest moments throughout the day to connect with your child. This means giving them a hug, making sure to say goodnight or goodbye to them. Once they start school, life starts to happen much more quickly, even more so than watching them crawl and then take their first steps and then learn their first words. Make sure to set a block of time sometime throughout the day to listen and communicate with your kids. I recommend always eating dinner at the dinner table. This way, you can enjoy a delicious meal and hear about everyone's days.

Commit to Being a Role Model

Whether you like it or not, the moment your child was born, you became an honorary role model. If you want to strive in raising kids that are respectful and considerate of you and others, even into their teen years, you must learn to treat them with the respect that you desire too. Even when you want to scream at them, take a deep breath and speak calmly and respectfully. It is important to learn how to manage your emotions, for you are showing your kids how to react to particular situations. Just remember, whatever made you angry, this too shall pass!

Commit to Teaching Emotional Intelligence

As a parent, you not only have to model the management of emotions, but you must know how to adequately teach it to your children too.

Teach self-soothing techniques. Even though we are told to let kids cry their tears out until they are tired, this really doesn't do too much good in the long run. When babies cry, we naturally feel obligated to soothe them to calm them down. Feel-good hormones are at work here, solidifying neural pathways that build self-soothing hormones.

Communicate to them that they way they feel is understandable, but make sure to let them know the actions they take when they feel a certain way should be limited.

Step into the shoes of your child and empathize with their emotions.

Really take the time to listen to them when they express their feelings to you. More often than not, kids just need the safe feeling of their parents' love. The unfortunate part is that young children often are not yet equipped with the communication skills to adequately articulate how they are feeling, which is why they may act out.

Commit to Being Consciously Aware of Your Child's Behavior

Your child has a reason for every action they take, even ones that may drive you crazy. While their reason may not ring as a good one to you, you need to locate what is triggering them to behave in such a manner. Yelling does not change their behavior, trust me. As a parent, you must look closer at the underlying need in order to really change a person's overall behavior. Passively noticing problem areas will result in children who want to cooperate with you.

Commit to a Punish-Free Guidance

Children typically are well behaved in order to please us as their parents. That is why when we are constantly ridiculing them or hard-punishing them, they harden as humans. Positive parenting is all about addressing their needs rather than homing in on their bad behaviors. You must learn how to empathically set boundaries. This way, you will end up with well-behaved kids who want to act well.

Commit to an Attitude of Gratitude

As a parent, one of the hardest things to do is choose your battles wisely. With each negative interaction you have with your kids, you are using up valuable time that could be utilized in a more positive manner. Focus in things like they way your child treats their siblings and other people, versus her leaving her shoes in your walking zone. Learn to be grateful for the things they do that you do approve of, and you will find that with praise on these things, they will begin to conduct themselves in ways you always approve of.

Commit to Compassion and Self-Acceptance

In order to give love, you must give love to yourself! We can only love our kids as much as our own hearts can allow us to. It is important to feel comfortable stretching out that heart of yours. If you feel bad about something, forgive and love yourself. This simple action will transform numerous areas of your life.

Commit to Keeping a Perspective

Kids, just like adults, are bound to make mistakes. It is an inevitable part of life as a human being. This means that you need to realize that you will never be an absolutely perfect parent and that your children will never be perfect either. Embracing love allows everyone in the household to truly thrive. You must consciously make the choice to be patient and kind to growing children. Believe it or not, even teenagers need you and your loving guidance more than you know. It is hard work but when done right, it will allow everyone in your family to not just survive but thrive fruitfully! Taking steps towards positivity will lead you to an entirely new outlook on life!

Chapter 10: Discipline: What Type Of Parent Are You?

"Pick your toys us now or I'll throw them in the bin!"

"Pick your toys up James, I'm always having to do it for you, why can't you be like your cousin, his Mum doesn't have to keep asking!"

"James, pick your toys up please."

"James, can you please pick your toys up when you get some time?"

Which parent are you? Do you threaten your child, nag them, give clear instructions with the expectation they will do it or ask your child with the hope they may follow an instruction when and if they want to?

"Pick your toys us now or I'll throw them in the bin!" (Would be a comment made by an Authoritarian parent)

"Pick your toys up James, I'm always having to do it for you, why can't you be like your cousin, his Mum doesn't have to keep asking!" (A nagging parent!)

"James, pick your toys up please." (An Authoritative or Responsible Parent)

"James, can you please pick your toys up when you get some time?" (A Permissive Parent)

Children thrive on structure, boundaries and love. The Authoritative or Responsible Model is the best one to aspire to. Children actually prefer to have boundaries set for them as it makes them feel safe and gives them feelings of security. By using firm and positive discipline and following through with consequences, children learn how to behave in a responsible manner and become young people who we, as parents, can be proud of.

Another essential factor to consider is the respect that we can earn, simply by disciplining our children in a positive and consistent manner. This leads to much easier parenting, better control of our kids and raising children who have grown to love and respect us. Respect is worth its weight in gold but it has to be earned. The following advice demonstrates effective discipline techniques so you do get to reap the rewards of having gained respect from your kids.

How Firm Should You Be?

The ultimate aim is of course, to have well behaved children but certainly not to the degree that they don't put a foot out of line for fear of retribution from their parents (authoritarian). Kids need a chance to be kids and if they're disciplined by overpowering, constantly disapproving and critical parents who do not take into consideration their age or individual personality, then this can have very negative effects on their self worth, feelings of happiness and overall enjoyment of life.

How Permissive Should You Be?

On the other hand, being too permissive and allowing your child do and have whatever they want will create an obnoxious little monster who no-one wants to be around. This can also have the effect of your child becoming constantly demanding or even a tyrant with complete power, which can lead to very negative feelings from you and even a dislike for your own child.

Finding a Happy Balance (Authoritative or Responsible Model)

By being firm with your child and consistent with your expectations, they will soon learn that you mean what you say and the good behavior will follow. A calm, consistent and caring approach should be taken however, rather than using a manner that's totally authoritarian and mean.

By being friendly but firm, you can let your child know that inappropriate behavior or rudeness is unacceptable and that they are much nicer people when they're behaving appropriately. This firmness will teach your child how to get along with others in an acceptable manner so that they don't face being unpopular out in the real world. Spoiled kids who are used to getting their own way find it very difficult to make and keep friends.

It's essential to use a firm approach right from the beginning! If your child refuses to give another child back their toy or refuses to hop off a swing when it's time to go home, don't be afraid to be firm. Give your child a warning, e.g. "You can have one more turn then you have to return it." Or, "I'll push you 3 more times on the swing then we have to go home." But then be sure to follow through even if they become vocal, cry or complain. They must learn that you mean what you say.

Following through and being consistent is essential. Your child will then learn that you mean business and that there are rules and boundaries in place that have to be followed and accepted.

This will result in you feeling happy because you have control and because your child is behaving in an acceptable manner. Your child will also feel happy because they're allowed to have fun while maintaining the boundaries that are expected of them. Children also respond extremely well to positive feedback. Praising your child for their good behavior encourages this behavior to continue. All kids thrive on positive feedback and really do want their parents to be happy with them.

Physical Punishment

Physical methods such as hitting or smacking are unnecessary forms of discipline especially when you've managed to gain control through communicating consistent rules and boundaries. All too often, parents can reach their limits and react with physical forms of punishment. When we are angry we can say and do things that we don't mean, so try to keep calm. Smacking a child can lead to children thinking that it's ok to hit others to get what they want. The most effective form of discipline is to be firm, give clear messages and set very clear and consistent boundaries.

Consequences

Being consistent with consequences is essential. If rules are broken, then you must follow through with a consequence. It's important though to communicate consequences in advance, so your child understands what will happen if they do misbehave, e.g. "If you keep running through the house and being silly, you will have to go to your room for # minutes." Simply letting your child get away with poor behavior just sends the message that they can do it again – and they will! It often only takes one or two occasions where a consequence is followed through for your child to learn that you mean what you say and they will most likely not break that rule again.

If they do break the rule again or repeat the misbehavior, then increase the consequence. You could double the time-out. (Normal time-out should correspond to your child's age, e.g. 4years old – 4 minute time-out session). Keep doing this until they get the message that you are in charge.

No matter how hard it is to be firm and consistent, it really will make life so much easier for you as a parent because you'll have well behaved children who aren't constantly pushing the boundaries. They will follow the rules and the end result will be happy parents and happy kids.

If you have a child with a strong will or character, you will have to make sure that you are consistent and follow through

100% of the time. A list of rules can help, with the rules and consequences written down. Start with a couple of rules that you want your child to master (the ones that are annoying and disrupting your family the most). When they master those, add on other rules (one at a time) and master them before adding any more.

Chapter 11: Taking Care Of Yourself

How can you be the parent you need to be if you are not taking care of yourself? The answer is simple: You cannot. Being a parent is not only a huge responsibility, it is also an enormous job that requires you to be at the top of your game. If you do not take care of your health, both physical and mental, then you are not acting in the best interest of your children. Your children need for you to be healthy and happy.

It is a scientifically proven fact that people who eat a proper diet and exercise regularly have fewer health problems, more energy, and live longer. As a busy parent, it is sometimes difficult to find the time for proper diet and exercise. However, it takes far less time and effort to follow a good diet and exercise routine than to deal with the energy loss and potential illnesses that come from not doing so.

We all learned in elementary school that wee need to eat from the five basic food groups every day. The five basic food groups are: dairy products, fruits, vegetables, grains, and meats. Your goal should be to eat three meals every day made up of products from each of those groups. Consume as many organic portions of these groups as possible to reduce artificial ingredients. If you are a responsible parent, you should always have all the ingredients in your home because your child's diet requires the same basic ingredients.

Portion control is vital to a healthy diet. Even healthy foods can become toxic to your health if not consumed in moderation. Each food item has certain levels of vitamins, minerals, and other nutrients in them. Some vitamins and minerals can be hazardous in large doses. Although I am not a fan of children consuming a regular vegetarian or vegan diet, many parents are choosing to go this route. If you do choose this type of diet for your child, you have the added responsibility of ensuring your child consumes the nutrients that a diet without dairy and meat deprives their body of.

Now that we have covered the scientifically correct diet, we should all be consuming, let's talk about today's reality. Today's society, communities, and basic home life is not the same as it was just two or three decades ago. In today's world, most two-parent homes have two working parents. Most single-parent homes have the single parent working. Most people do not grow their own organic fruits and vegetables or raise their own dairy and meat sources. Most parents have precious little time to cook one or two meals, let alone three meals a day for their family.

Substitution is key in today's world. If you do not have time to prepare a full, five-course meal three times a day, substitute the meals with the most nutritious and healthy quick-fix foods you can find. Most grocery stores sell microwaveable sausage patties and links, ready-cooked bacon, pre-sliced fruit, microwaveable eggs, quick-grits, easy-fix oatmeal, and cereals with low sugar and high grain contents. A nutritious breakfast will set the stage for a more successful day.

Lunch does not need to be a hassle. If you have a busy day and cannot prepare a home-cooked meal for lunch, there are healthy alternatives. A basic sandwich and chips provide some basic fuel for your body but does not provide it with the kinds of nutrients you need to keep your body functioning at peak performance. Try making sure you add fruit and vegetables to every lunch, even if the portions are small.

The goal for supper should be to have a quiet, slow, sit-down gathering with all the family. Spend some time online to research easy dishes that require minimum ingredients, maximum flavors, and minimum cook times. The less time you spend cooking means you will have more time to enjoy the meal and communicate with your family.

When you find yourself too busy to prepare and consume the recommended daily diet, substitutions with supplements is the next best thing. Most medical professionals recommend a daily dietary supplement, even for those who eat a balanced and healthy diet. Supplementals can be purchased in the form of a daily vitamin pill or in flavored drinks. Either way, adding the extra supplements to your existing diet will add fuel to your body and mind.

Daily exercise is crucial to a healthy body and mind. Exercise causes your body to release endorphins. Endorphins aid in your mental health and overall mood. As a parent with children who have boundless energy, exercising regularly will help you to have the strength, energy, and stamina to keep up with your active children.

Finding time to exercise is a challenge for anyone in today's busy world, especially if you have children. However, instead of using your parenting responsibilities as an excuse NOT to exercise, use them as part of your exercise routine. Getting your children involved in your exercise routine is healthy and fun for each of you. You will get the physical benefits that make you both stronger and create a stronger parent/child bond at the same time.

If your child is in a stroller, use that to your advantage. You can take brisk walks while pushing your child in the stroller. You benefit from the walk, your child benefits from spending time with you, and you both benefit from the fresh air, sunshine, and the outdoor environment. If your child is too big for a stroller you can choose to find simple activities that you can both enjoy outdoors. Consider playing a game of tag, hide-and-seek, or tossing a ball. Just remember to dress yourself and your child appropriately for the weather, remain in shaded areas as much as possible, and keep hydrated.

If you choose to exercise without your child, find a time during the day or evening that your child is at school or busy with some other activity, such as doing homework, or after they have gone to bed. Some people find it more beneficial to exercise without the distraction of their children. The goal should be to find 15-30 minutes for an exercise routine. If a daily routine is simply not a possibility, at least find the time to exercise three times a week to ensure your body gets the attention needed to remain healthy.

Exercise is supposed to help you and not meant to hurt you. Do not over-do it. If you overexert yourself and cause harm to your body, there is nothing beneficial to your heath or to your children in that. Start out with a simple routine three times a week. Whatever your choice of exercise routine, you should walk away from it feeling both tired and rejuvenated at the same time. Gradually increase the intensity and duration of your routine until you have the desired routine that fits into your lifestyle. The routine should be fun and something you look forward to. Remember, exercise will only become a habit if it is fun for you, so find a routine that makes exercising fun for yourself.

All parents need to spend some time away from their children. It does not make you a bad parent to desire time alone or time to be with others. Although you are a parent, you are also an individual. You do not have to relinquish your entire individual identity when you become a parent.

It is healthy to let go. When your children are in your care you are required to be responsible for every detail of their lives. Your own life often gets put aside or placed on hold. That is not healthy for yourself or your children. You, as a parent, need to retain your identity as a person. Your child needs to see that you are more than just a parent.

Spending time away from your children shows them that you are a well-rounded individual and will allow your child to respect you as a person. You will be setting the stage to allowing your child to become an individual with interests of their own. Time away from your children also makes the reunion exciting and enjoyable.

Your lifestyle and the ages of your children will dictate the amount of time you need to be separated from them. Some parents enjoy a few hours a week away from their children while others find it healthy to leave their children with trusted adults and take a week-long vacation on a regular basis. Finding time for yourself and to remain an individual should strengthen your relationship with your children and not diminish it.

As discussed in an earlier segment, it is your responsibility as a parent to ensure your children are placed with competent and reliable adults when they are not in your care. Every family is different with unique dynamics. Ideally, you will have caring and responsible family members who will care for your children so that you can find time for yourself. However, that is not always the case. Some parents have reliable friends or trusted neighbors they can count on. As a last resort, some parents can afford to hire a responsible adult to care for their children. No matter your situation or available resources, it falls on you to ensure your children are with someone who will care for their needs and be responsible in your absence.

Once you have acquired proper childcare for your children, go have fun and revisit your life as an individual. Take the time to go to the movies and see a film that does not have cartoon characters in it. Go shopping for something besides groceries. Take a trip to visit an old friend or a relative you have not had contact within a while. Spend the day relaxing on the beach without having to constantly chase your child. Go sit in a quiet park and read a book. Spend the day at a spa. Whatever you do with your free time, relax and make the time all about you. The happier you are, the happier your child will be.

Alcohol and drugs are the number one reason children are removed from their parents in the United States. This chapter has detailed the importance of taking care of yourself in order to make yourself the best parent you can be for your children. If you are under the influence of drugs or alcohol you are not being the best parent you can be. You deserve a better life that these chemicals allow you to have and your children deserve a parent that is not a slave to the chemicals in these substances.

Alcohol and drug abuse causes mood swings, anger outbursts, slow reaction time, irritability, prolonged sleep, poor judgement, and countless physical and mental disorders. You cannot be a responsible and reliable parent to you children if you are under the influence of drugs or alcohol. When you use alcohol or drugs as a parent, you are choosing to put your selfish wants before your child's needs. If you are abusing any substance, you need to seek professional help. Most abusers cannot stop using on their own. Some substances are dangerous to stop using without proper help. If you are abusing substances and decide you want a better life for yourself and your family, seek help from a reputable treatment provider who provides holistic treatment.

Getting proper medical care for yourself is something you owe your children. Most insurance plans have a free yearly basic physical as part of their coverage for individuals. The reason for this is that studies have shown that early detection of most diseases and conditions are less expensive to treat and more likely to be less fatal than if the disease or condition goes undetected for a long period of time.

When you get sick, it is important for you to seek medical help. If you contract a virus and do not treat it, chances are your children will contract the virus as well. If you do not have medical insurance and cannot afford regular healthcare, your local county Health Department will provide care and base the cost on your income. If you are on public assisted healthcare, you owe it to the taxpayers to take good care of yourself. If you are receiving assistance with your healthcare, chances are most of the funds paying for your assistance comes from people who must pay much higher prices for their family's healthcare. It is responsible citizenship to take good care of yourself.

Get a good night's sleep. Only a fraction of us get the recommended eight hours of sleep each night. If you are one of the millions of busy adults who fail to get the recommended sleep each night, start focusing on your sleep routine. Whatever your typical bedtime is right now, make it a point to move that time up by 15-30 minutes each night until you are sleeping a full 8 hours. You will find it easier and more rewarding to wake up fully rested, refreshed, and ready to start your child's day off properly after a good night's sleep.

A happier person is a healthier person. Happiness breeds happiness. Seek out and find happy people that enjoy the same things you enjoy. Seek out up-beat people who value family and healthy living. Attend a church that enlightens you and makes you feel good. Watch comedy films. When your children see your happiness, they are happier.

Children require constant care. To be a responsible parent, you need to be in good physical and mental health to provide the care your children need. If you are not living a healthy lifestyle, start today to make the necessary changes to fix that. Set realistic goals for your improvements. As with all aspects of parenting, you will face many obstacles and setbacks. Expect those setbacks so that you are not blindsided and discouraged by them. When the setbacks happen, pick yourself up and start where you left off. Responsible parenting is the hardest job in the world with benefits that cannot be measured.

Chapter 12: Does It Make Sense To Praise A Child Often?

We become victims of generalities. How should we measure the strictness volume: in kilograms or liters? I want to review specific situations.

At What Moment You Should Switch to

Your Strictness Mode? To What Extent?

If a child is praised, he starts to feel that if he does not cope with a task, he will be blamed. The praise always has a reverse side: recognition means evaluation. Perhaps, you are familiar with the concept' non-evaluative attitude to a child.' What does it mean? It means no evaluative approach to a child but not to his actions. You may have heard that you should criticize/praise a child's activities but not a child himself. Don't say, you're 'wrong, you're smart' but say, 'I like the way you said, the way you did.' 'This deed is not very good, and you certainly know that this deed is not very good, so next time you'll try to act better, won't you?'. After criticism, it is helpful to add some positive remarks.

Moreover, you cannot correct the behavior in critical situations. When a child has done something and feels that he is affected by some emotion, you should never alter his behavior. If you punish him, he won't change nonetheless. Emotional reasons should be revealed and, desirably, neutralized, but in a quiet atmosphere.

I will give you a specific example from life.

A mother has a question,

'My kid is nine years old. The situation at school is as follows: two children sit at one desk, and one of them doesn't like when someone takes his belongings, starts crying and scratching, and my son knows it but keeps doing these things anyway. I start talking to him; he stares into my eyes and can't explain why he acts so.'

'Well, that's a concert! Why should he explain anything to you, it's you who has to explain things to him', I answered?

Mother,

'This is what I keep telling! I am saying, 'You see Steve…''

Such phrases are parents' reflexes originating from a culture, from the understanding of upbringing as imposing our norms, requirements to a child without constructing any dialogue with him. Thus, first, we must accept the child and ensure active listening.

Chapter 13: Respect

Respect can be one of the most difficult lessons to provide to your child. Respect is about showing manners and courtesy despite your impulses. There are times when impatience will want to win you over, but you have to fight against all of the negative emotions you want to let out. If you display inappropriate behaviors or bad manners, your children are going to start adopting these behaviors too. It comes down to being aware of your actions and doing the right thing even when it is difficult. Try to lead by example, don't tell your child "do as I say, not as I do." Your child isn't going to understand why it is ok for you to do some things, but they cannot. Telling your child, "because I am the adult," is not a good enough reason.

Your Actions Should Speak Louder

As the adult, you need to teach respect through your actions and set an example for your child When you are in a situation that tests your patience, think about people who work as customer service representatives (CSR).If you have ever worked in this industry you understand exactly what this means.Anyone who hasworked as a server or behind a retail counter knows how much patience it takes to keep a positive attitude and keep smiling even when you want to tell the customer to leave and never come back.

The training you received when you were young can be also used as a parent, but if you have never worked in customer service you may want to take a course.The best time to do this is before your child turns one year old. The reason for this is because your child will pick up more from you after this age. Of course, your child is already watching you as a baby, but when they learn words in conjunction with body language, you will have more work to do in creating a positive environment.

There are customer service style courses that can teach you how to react in trying situations. You can also visit a therapist to gain more insight.Any method you find helpful in gaining insight is helpful as long as it helps you maintain a more positive, patient attitude.

Customer service representatives are taught to:

Listen

Think

Assess what the real problem is

Analyze the options you have to correct the problem

Provide empathy

Provide a solution

If you can follow these steps while keeping a calm appearance and body language, then you will be able to use your actions to show your child respect. This will then help your child learn respect from you.

This process is also about treating others how you would like to be treated versus how they are treating you.

Understanding How Your Child Wants to Be Treated

Your child wants respect, that is a given, but they may not understand have to give and receive respect correctly if they do not have a good example to follow. If they see you disrespecting others who are disrespectful to you, they may think this is the correct way to respond. They may learn that receiving disrespect means you give it back. This negative situation makes it harder to teach your child that it is not appropriate.

Your child will always look to you to provide an example on how to act and behave. You will always need to treat others how you wish to be treated, thus you have to give respect even when another may not deserve it.

You can also explain to your child that you want to be treated kindly. You can use the example that you have treated them with nothing but kindness, so you require the same in return.

Another way to handle the situation is to ask your child if they like it when they are treated poorly or when someone disrespects them. This can be a good starting point to talk about the right way to give and receive respect too. Of course, there will be times when your child tests their boundaries, but if you can provide a consistent example by being respectful in all situations you will gain respect from your child and teach a valuable lesson in the process.

This does not mean that you allow yourself to be a doormat. It is possible to stand up for yourself and remain respectful to another person. That is the ultimate lesson to teach your child.

You may wish to repeat the following statement to yourself if you are having trouble with the concept of being assertive yet respectful. Tell yourself, "I have treated you with nothing but kindness. I am not asking for your appreciation but I am asking that you respect me as another human being."Affirming this statement to yourself will mean that it becomes a mantra and something you remember when dealing with others who are not as respectful as you want them to be. Your child will learn an amazing amount of behavior and mannerisms from you as a parent.This is why it is important for you to learn to control your own reactions, impulses and behavior in front of them.Being a good role model is key to helping your child learn how to respond appropriately in any situation.

If you wish to be a positive parent, then practice, practice, and practice some more.Only through practice can we make these things become a habit.Once they are a habit it is easy to show our children how to give and receive respect as well as how to ask for it when necessary.

Only when you give respect freely, without expecting anything in return, can you get it back in return.If you demand respect without giving it first, then there is no reason for your child to learn respect from you or to give it to you.

An Exercise for Building Respect

Manners are incredibly important and they are the first step to receiving respect from other people no matter what the situation.Begin by using please, thank you, excuse me, and other words that communicate respect to those around you.When interacting with employees in a store or restaurant, use these words, especially in front of your child.You can also use them with your spouse.Showing gratitude for something your spouse has done is a great way to create a lesson of respect for your child.

You can also work on controlling your responses to certain situations. This is critical to do before your child becomes older since these behaviors will become a habit as they age. For example, if you are in traffic, try not to verbally express your frustration. Avoid yelling at other drivers or getting angry if someone cuts you off. Keep your thoughts to yourself or distract yourself with another activity such as singing along to the radio. Another good way to distract yourself is to talk to your child as you drive or remember a funny story. Refocus on the good things or happier times and you can refocus your attention while staying respectful of other people.

Chapter 14: Patient Parenting

Parenting requires constant work and positive thinking as your toddler becomes more active. The curiosity of a child can become overwhelming. You can keep a loving and positive attitude by taking the extra time and continue to build the bond between each of you—the parent and child. You must work through the obstacles faced together as a team. Everyone has limits, and that doesn't make anyone a bad parent, it makes you normal.

Listening to what your toddler is attempting to tell you can sometimes be a difficult chore. With the additional love and support of you as the parental figure, the child will continue to adapt and learn.

The trust will develop as each of you continues working on daily problems until you have a workable solution to any situation faced in the day of a toddler. Unfortunately, the well planned map is constantly changing.

Self-Soothing a Child

Once again, kind-heartedness goes a long way, and a crying baby is a good indication of something the child is lacking. Many years ago, parents believed if the child is fed, clean, and warm was all that was necessary. Let the child cry was the logic used. However, it has been proven that soothing a child is part of a physiological process.

If a child is crying, a parent can help the child's peaceful responses since oxytocin and other comforting biochemical are released during the nurturing process.

Biologically, the child is setting the neural pathways for hormones to help self-soothing when he/she is upset.

You need to listen actively to what the child is saying or simulating. It is not always evident why the child was acting out, so you need to gather the facts before you decide punishment is the road to take. A loving hug could be all that is required to make the cranky child a happy child.

Reasons a Child Acts Out

It is essential to discover what has your child so out of sorts. A young child cannot communicate effectively, so it is up to you.

Children display emotions in many ways—but acting out is not a pretty sight. Professionals believe it is excellent therapy to take pictures of your child when he/she is acting out for whatever reason. Show the child the picture of what he or she looks like when happiness versus sadness is created.

For older children, the pictures can serve as a feelings chart so he or she can decide which face fits his/her mood. This is an easier method to relay to children when you are so frustrated and have no words readily available. It is as simple as showing the child how inappropriate the facial expressions are when he/she is angry or upset.

Keep the pictures handy for any unexpected event when you cannot quickly remedy the situation or its cause. That picture can be worth a thousand words.

Eliminate Stressful Situations

It isn't always possible to eradicate stressful situations with a toddler. You have probably figured out what trigger points to look for with your child. Many of those times include bedtime, mealtime, and naptime. These are happy times but if you have errands to complete outside of the home; plan ahead.

Have you ever taken a sleepy or hungry child to the grocery store? If your answer is yes, you realize it is best to go when a child is not tired or hungry, but sometimes it's unavoidable. Be sure you have an emergency supply of snacks and a cuddly toy in case your little one decides to take a nap to or from the journey to the store.

Avoid situations where you will have to rush about with your kid because all it usually does is add more frustration to your trip. It is okay to think out loud and inform your youngster of an upcoming date with the grocery store. He/she might understand more than you realize. Try any approaches within reason to maintain a tranquil atmosphere.

Think like a Youngster

By providing choices, you are allowing your young person to become involved in a decision by using positive approaches. For example, some kids hate car seats. Begin the conversation of how you know and understand that he/she doesn't like the seat but it will keep him/her safe.

Ask your kid which favorite toy or book he/she wants to take for an outing or which snack should be packed for the outing. Involve your child, and you might be surprised at the results. Make the outing an adventure.

Recognize Your Impatience

Emotions can run high when a toddler is acting out to get attention. The auto button switches on when a parent becomes overwhelmed. The stress adds up until you believe you are a bad parent and need to be more patient.

Gather that emotion and become proactive to turn the thought around. Recognize your weakness and continue to improve your patience levels. It is all a part of the continuing process of coping with a newborn baby or a toddler.

Take a step back if the child is old enough to understand or give it a short time and let the child know you will discuss the bad behavior in a few minutes. This break will also teach the toddler everyone needs a moment to regroup when poor behavior is used.

Not everyone agrees with this method, but your child might learn a small amount of dread by having to wait. Both the child and parent need a break once in a while.

Diagnose Your Impatience

You need to diagnose when you are losing your patience and make an attempt to correct the trigger point. Emotions are tricky, and your impatience levels are sure signs that a problem exists. Is there a reason your days seem to be filled with aggravation? Parents are only human, and it would be a strange event if they don't react to the drama occasionally.

Schemes of bad behavior could be an indication your child needs to have a bit more one on one time with you. Maybe it is time to spend a little more time with the child if whining is persistent or if the child is clinging to you all day.

Nurture the child and you might not need to think of ways to punish him/her for any acts of misconduct. The child's acting out could be a reaction stemming from your impatience.

Make New Commitments

It is possible to get in a rut and not know how you got there which can result in overreacting to a child's needs or desires. Begin your day with a positive outlook and it should reflect upon your child. It requires reprogramming your subconscious mind to place you in a more tranquil setting.

Make an effort to speak with other parents who have similar issues with a child. You will begin to realize, it is also you and not just the child that needs some correctional methods.

Begin by taking better care of yourself by eating healthy and getting sufficient rest. Of course—with a newborn or toddler—

you might want to engage in a nap when he/she has one.

If you are rested, you will be less likely to transmit a negative mood onto your child. By slowing down, you are more focused and won't look at your child as a problem. Enjoy the time you have and you might be surprised how happy your toddler becomes without the stressful yelling matches.

Take a Break

Parenthood can be overwhelming, and you may need some extra time to reboot. If you emotions are running high, it may take a few minutes to release the strong emotions of a whining baby. You need to cleanse your agitated thoughts until they become more rational.

If you have some backup, it is best to use them until you can recover your composure. It could take approximately 30 minutes or more to calm completely down. Use the one minute approach (explained later) if you are alone or count to ten.

While you are counting, focus on your breathing techniques to slow down your anxiety levels. Slow breathing can help you calm down and makes your brain be removed of the apprehension felt when your child became agitated.

Observe Your Responses

When your aggravation levels rise, you will notice physical signs such as sweaty palms, feel hot, have difficulty breathing, or notice an increased heart rate. Physical signs cannot be ignored because they could cause you to overreact.

Each element involved with a crying infant or toddler can create these symptoms. It only means this is another part of the puzzle needed to understand your responses to your child. Your patience levels are wearing thin, and you need the time-out to regroup your thoughts.

Feed on the Good Days

If a child can get your attention in a positive way, you might not need to referee the next toddler fight. When your child has a play date, it is a good way to interact with other children. If the child has been troublesome in the past, you should praise all of the good play times when the youngsters are content. The content pattern is a good indication that your plans concerning discipline are functional.

All it takes is a smile, a hug, or a pat on the back to let your child know everything is doing great. It also is a good indication to the child that he/she is doing what makes his/her parents happy. The praise is received so you can carry on with your household duties without the loud yelling matches.

Enthusiasm and praise will let the adolescent know how happy you are with his/her actions, and happiness is also contagious. You can prepare a reward system, but it doesn't need to be something purchased from the store. The treat can be a game played, or a book read quietly with Mom, Dad, or another caregiver. Make it a special surprise, not just the one favorite book you read before bedtime.

Take Time for Self-Care

Time grows thin when you become agitated or upset with your kid, but you still have to take care of yourself—the parent—if you expect to take care of an infant or toddler. You cannot be patient with your busy child if you are overloaded and feel underappreciated. All parents and caregivers have levels of patience which can be stretched to the max before we realize it.

As a successful adult, we have learned steady perseverance is what is needed with a youngster, so you can handle the hard stuff faced even if you feel like throwing in the towel for the day. By setting aside just ten minutes each day for your special time, can make a difference everyone will notice.

Self-Care Ideas for Your Mind

Of course, you are probably saying who has the time? It only takes a few moments to find an escape while you are handling your daily tasks with your child. As with any other discipline plan, it takes time when making a plan and forming a daily habit or routine.

Get goofy: Your child demands and requires your attention at all times. Parenting doesn't need to be a stuffy routine you face every day. Get silly and have some fun whether it is directed at your kid or if you are looking in a mirror.

Make a list: If you aren't taking the extra time to take care of yourself, try making a list of little things you can do during the day that might put a smile on your face.

Take some pictures: Take five minutes out of your routine to look at some photos or snap a few new ones. A cute face from your baby will surely cheer you up.

Get some assistance: You won't be considered weak or a bad parent if you get a nanny or housekeeper to help you out once in a while. Not only will it give you a break, but your child might enjoy it also. Bringing a fresh approach to the mix might be all that is needed to console a child and prevent any disciplinary actions.

De-stress your mind and body by taking a walk: Get a friend or someone else to watch your baby during naptime so you can clear your thoughts. Sometimes, just staring into the sky can help with your patience levels.

Self-Care Ideas for Your Body

As a parent of a newborn or toddler, you will become tired quickly if you are not accustomed to the rigorous routines involved with raising a healthy and happy child. It is essential to take extra steps to remain healthy and ready for whatever faces you and your youngster.

In some ways, your child can also enjoy some of the benefits of the procedures you use to become healthier. It goes back to the adage whereas if Mom isn't happy, no one is happy!

Eat healthier: Create healthier breakfast, lunch, and dinner choices. A balanced diet goes a long way to increasing your tolerance levels. Don't forget to add a special treat occasionally. You deserve some rewarding too.

Turn on some tunes: If your child is awake, turn up the music and dance around for a few minutes. Include your child in the dance whether you are holding him/her or just jumping around together. Your body needs the focused cardio input.

Consume some electromagnetic energy: Sunlight is the answer because it contains photons which are packets of energy. Just a few minutes of its warmth can adjust the worst of moods, especially on those days when nothing appears to make you or your kid happy.

Inhale pleasant aromas: As easy as it seems, you will find when you bake a yummy cake or cook a fabulous meal the odor lingers. The tantalizing aroma will provide a temporary escape. If you don't have a meal in the making, simply place some cinnamon or peppermint oil in a pan of water on the stove or a crock pot and reap the benefits.

Choose to have a good laugh: It doesn't matter whether it is a book, television, or another resource; it is essential to be happy.

As you practice these self-help methods, the responsibilities of raising your youngster, won't seem as daunting. The small pleasures will provide the necessary escape to deal with whatever your kid attempts to accomplish—good or bad. You have to be fine-tuned just like your automobile so you can continue with the discipline needed for your child; no matter what his/her age is at the time.

Chapter 15: Know Thy Child

Now this step will follow you for the rest of your life actually.You will need to be attentive and get to know what your child is up to at all stages of his life.By knowing your child, his health conditions, his mental development stage and his personality, you will be able to become a better parent and create a favorable environment for him.Different children have different needs.Even siblings can be totally different and that's why, as a parent, you should really take the time to learn all about your child as an individual, and be interested in every aspect of his or her life.

A great way to get to know your child and better understand him, is to observe him.This applies for any age.Sit down and look at your child as he is playing, eating and sleeping. You can already discern a lot about their personality at a young age. Are they contented or do they need to be entertained all the time? What seems to be their favorite activity throughout the day? Your children will also communicate a lot of precious information to you by their body language and facial expressions, so pay attention. It is very difficult for children to express their feelings, so by being aware of their nonverbal responses or cues, you can discern how they feel regarding specific situations or events.

As they get older, you can ask them specific questions. However, you will find out that children answer better when they don't feel interrogated. So, instead of always asking the same question "what did you learn in school today? Ask them specifics. Get familiar with the school program and the typical activities and ask them precise questions."How was the meat loaf and mashed potatoes from the cafeteria today?What position did you play at your basketball game today?I know you had a field trip today, where did you sit on the bus on your way there?How is your friend Terry who usually sits next to you in your Spanish class doing?

It's also very important to be in touch with the people in your child's life.Meet their friends and their friend's parents.Communicate on a regular basis with their teacher or school counselor.Check in with your relatives or babysitters to see if they notice the same changes or behaviors if you are worried about something. All of this could greatly assist in you better knowing your child.

By observing your child and being involved in his life as much as possible, you will develop a solid bond.You will also be able to identify and correct certain behaviors if needed.For example, if your child develops an aggressive behavior all of the sudden, you might need some time to find out what is bothering him.Remember that your child will be greatly influenced by your behavior, so make sure that if you are seeing undesirable behavior in him or her, it is not simply a repetition of yours.For example, it is really common for children with parents going through a divorce to be aggressive or depressed.They are most likely exposed to fights during difficult times and torn between two parents they love equally.Make sure you always try to explain to your children at their level what's happening.

Make time for your children.These days, most parents have to work long hours and between the piano lessons and the homework, quality time is difficult to fit in.Don't forget that you only have your children at home for a relatively short period of their lives and that you should try to make the most of it every day.Set some time aside, to have a one on one bonding time with your child.If you have several children, it is essential that you plan some one on one activities at times, in order to connect directly with the child without distraction.This will make them feel special and they will more easily open up to you if something is bothering them.

Chapter 16: Self-Esteem, The Great Misunderstanding

The definition of self-esteem has become slippery over the last few decades, with the rise of the self-esteem movement in the United States. The term self-esteem was first used and defined in 1892 by William James, who wrote that self-esteem was a summation of a person's view and development of self which allowed them to adapt in social situations with an appropriate projection of self. He said that self-esteem, when honed correctly, was vital to success and achievement. This new idea of the importance of self-esteem in children combined with the view that children were frail and needed to be protected led to an onslaught of further studies that explored the link and possible causal connection between self-esteem in childhood and academic and professional success later in life.

As the psychology of child development gained traction in the early and mid twentieth century, and along with it the view of the causal relationship between self-esteem and academic success, more school teachers hopped on board with the idea of creating supportive school programs that sought to promote good self-esteem in children in their classrooms through positive reinforcement and rejection of some of the old methods of negative reinforcement.

In 1967, Stanley Coopersmith identified a correlation between self-esteem and frailty, saying that, "in children domination, rejection, and severe punishment result in lowered self-esteem." This was followed by a series of changes in schools. Students were encouraged to participate in non-academic activities, like service work, in order to help them explore other things they might be good at and which might contribute to their self-esteem. Instead of calling on students to recite facts to show their knowledge, teachers encouraged them to make up skits and perform them or to show what they were learning in other more creative ways like through art or computers.

These initial changes were new and exciting, because they allowed students to embrace a variety of different interests, including the nonacademic disciplines. But it went one step further. Teachers were encouraged to leave positive remarks on all graded papers along with, and sometimes instead of, the critical feedback. Sometimes, grades were done away with altogether out of fear that a child who didn't do well might feel bad about himself. This rampant concern for self-esteem led, undoubtedly, to the grade inflation that we see today in many schools. Today it's common for students to be graded not on the quality of their work, but on their effort, two things that don't necessarily coincide.

In their paper on self-esteem, Heatherton and Wyland say that, "Having high self-esteem apparently provides benefits to those who possess it: They feel good about themselves, they are able to cope effectively with challenges and negative feedback, and they live in a social world in which they believe that people value and respect them" (2003). They follow this up by saying that very high self-esteem can have negative consequences. Such consequences can include being overly defensive, egotistical, arrogant, complacent, and lacking in empathy for others. In twenty-first century America, we are seeing the consequences more clearly than ever before.

The Self-Esteem Movement

In 1969, psychologist Nathaniel Brandon published a paper called "The Psychology of Self-Esteem." This paper made the assertion that "feelings of self-esteem were the key to success in life." The Coopersmith paper and many others before and after it inspired the self-esteem movement that swept through the United States.

California schools were the first to implement a program that required teachers to teach self-esteem to students. They were required to follow a curriculum that would remind students that they are unique and special. A writer from the New York Times in 1986 joked that, "There are those who believe that the [self-esteem task force] is an excellent example of a certain geographical eccentricity." The same article quoted Dr. Roy Christman saying, "It sounds so California. I can't imagine Idaho having a task force on self-esteem."

Armed with correlations between high self-esteem and success, this well-meaning movement sought to improve everything from societal problems like teen pregnancy, drug and alcohol abuse, and high divorce rates, to academic problems like low test scores. What the proponents of this movement didn't take into account was that the strong positive correlation found between self-esteem and success signified that self-esteem and success are related but not that self-esteem creates success.

Richard Lee Colvin, a Los Angeles Times writer wrote that one particular school in California began to implement daily "I love me" lessons in which students repeated sentences like "I am gifted" until they memorized them. Other classes would have students stand in front of the class while their classmates had to say nice things about them and cheer for them.

It's become rare for students to get through a school day without hearing phrases like, "To succeed, you must believe in yourself," and, "If you can dream it, you can do it." Many a middle school kid has rolled his eyes at these statements, and rightfully so, because in real life, dreams and belief in oneself are not enough.

Years later, this movement has swept across the nation, test scores are lower than ever before, and self-esteem, or perhaps more accurately, egotism, is at an all-time high. Numerous studies on self-esteem have been done comparing self-esteem and test scores of American children with children in other countries who do not place such an emphasis on self-esteem. One such study found that self-esteem did not seem to have a positive influence on test scores. In fact, though American children had the highest reported self-esteem, they scored much lower on math testing than students in Japan and Korea, whose self-esteem was not nearly as high (SOURCE). It turns out that happiness and feelings of self worth by themselves don't make people smarter.

Instead of making kids smarter, the self-esteem movement has been found to do one of two things. It gives children an inflated sense of their own abilities and entitlement that leaves them ill-prepared to handle professional criticism later on in their lives, or it leads them to believe that when adults give them praise they never mean it, and thus never take any praise seriously, which in turn does not promote self-esteem, but does quite the opposite.

In fact, much of the self-esteem movement has served to screw kids up more than it has helped them. While in the past, self-esteem has been more accurately defined in terms of a child's feelings of self worth in relation to peers, school, family, and different activities, this evolved definition of self-esteem operates from the assumption that young children, even toddlers, are capable of abstract thought like uniqueness and individuality, and moreover, that when a child experiences feelings of low self-esteem it is always a bad thing.

Dr. Thomas Phelan, the psychologist and father of two who wrote the 1-2-3 Magic

Program, defines healthy self-esteem as coming from four basic categories: good relationships with other people, competence in work and self-management, physical skills and caring for one's body, and character (which includes courage, effort, following the rules, and concern for others). In his video talk, he goes on to elaborate on each of these categories, explaining that the dissonance a child feels in each category at any given time is a natural part of growing up. For example, fourteen-year-old Norah hates brushing her hair. She doesn't see the point of doing it, so she doesn't do it. One day, a classmate makes fun of her messy hair, and a bunch of kids laugh at her. Norah is hurt and embarrassed. As a result, she has incentive to start regularly brushing her hair.

Some experts argue that when a child is allowed to feel bad about herself, it's often a motivating factor toward self improvement. A child who is never allowed to feel bad about herself will feel a lot less intrinsic motivation to improve. After all, who spends time improving what they think they have already mastered?

Rather than high self-esteem causing success in life, it's highly probable that success in life causes high self-esteem. When Max finally masters his fractions, he is filled with a genuine, lasting sense of accomplishment that makes him feel good about himself. Had his teacher told him that he's great no matter what, even if he can't understand fractions, he might still have felt okay about himself, but not nearly as good as he does when he's allowed to struggle with the tough concept and attain mastery over it. Struggle and disappointment are necessary ingredients to success both in the present and in the future. With this in mind, it's ironic that so many educational institutions have tried to eliminate the struggle from the studies.

Some schools have banned the use of red pens to correct papers, reasoning that red is an aggressive color that makes negative feedback feel worse for children. Competitive activities for younger children are often frowned upon, because competition means that there have to be winners and losers, and a young child will feel bad about himself if he loses.

Victor, a stay at home father of a preschooler in T-ball was shocked when he went to his son's game and saw that they didn't play with three outs—the little players batted through the order no matter how many outs there were, so that everyone got a turn. "That wasn't the most surprising thing," he said. "The strangest thing was at the end when everyone, even the kids on the losing team, was handed ribbons for their effort. That would never have happened when I was a kid. We were expected to just deal with losing. Yeah, losing sucks, but it's not the worst thing out there."

Victor brings up an interesting point—it used to be that children were allowed to lose, and parents could use it as a teaching tool. What's happening? Are our best intentions screwing up our kids?

Implications Today

Today it's easy to equate self-esteem with ego. The two are nothing alike. A child with a healthy level of self-esteem will have a realistic perspective of himself. Having a high ego just means that he's good at thinking in self-centered ways.

What school administrators forget is that they are not the primary influencers of a child's self-esteem; a child's parents are. If a child is so fragile that a teacher giving him honest critical feedback on his homework is going to shatter his self-esteem, then there are most likely problems going on at home that should be addressed, rather than ignored while teachers walk on eggshells around him. The self-esteem movement has left major marks on the ways in which parents discipline and educate their children.

Marlene, a mother of two young daughters says that she always feels scared to discipline her children in public. "Cleo smacks Lilly in the beauty parlor, and when I turn around to tell her to stop it, I wonder if the mothers around me think I'm being too harsh on her. After all, she's only four, and she is pretty darn cute. I know Cleo knows that hitting is not allowed, but anyone sitting there can assume anything they want about me.

What if they assume Cleo's hitting Lilly because that's what I do at home? Of course that's not true, but sometimes I fear they might think that. Women can be so judgmental, especially when it comes to children."

Marlene went on to describe another time she was out with the girls. Lilly had started crying huge alligator tears in the checkout line at the gas station because Marlene had told her no treats this time. Lilly folded her arms around herself and shuffled behind her mother. "She was clearly just pouting, which I was ready to ignore, but then the lady in line ahead of us informed me rather loudly that she didn't see why I felt I had to upset my child like this. Clearly she was distraught about not getting a treat when she was being so good.

I was taken aback. Was she right? Was I just being mean? Was not getting her treats very often going to hurt her self-esteem? It sounds so stupid and small, but maybe it's true," she said. "I bought the treat, and Lilly perked up and told me I was the best mom in the world and she loved me very much. The lady in front of me watched the whole thing with a satisfied smirk. 'Now doesn't that feel good?' she asked me, as if I was the child, and she'd just taught me a life-changing lesson. It didn't feel good. It felt like I'd been manipulated. Now Lilly will expect that her pouting will cause me to change my mind again in the future."

There's a pervasive fear among many Americans that telling kids no and making them wait for things will damage their self-esteem. The truth is that a child's self-esteem is not so fragile that it is contingent upon one yes or no question in the checkout line at the gas station.

Conclusion

Thank you for reading this book until the end. I hope that it inspires and guides you on your parenting journey.

Remember that parenting is not a marathon or a sprint. It requires time, practice, determination, right skills, and perseverance to get the golden ticket – a respectful, well-mannered child. It is not a competition that you play with other parents. It is building a personal relationship with your child.

Parenting is about providing loving guidance with great purpose- to mold the character and personality of your child. It is about understanding who he is, what he cares about, what are his dreams, what brings him happiness or sadness, and what are his strengths and weaknesses. It is about focusing your time and attention to what matters to him while keeping limitations and boundaries.

Parenting is also learning about yourself as a nurturer, a disciplinarian, a confidant, and many other roles associated with it. If you make mistakes or feel your patience running out, take a time-out, and relax. You become a fine parent when you are happy, calm, and centered. Your health and well-being matters because it helps you become an objective, affectionate, and positive parent.

By being present and aware, your child is also empowering you and teaching you how to become a better person. When you know who you are, you become more capable of helping him understand himself. And when your child knows himself in the deepest sense, he is more confident to manage the challenges that come his way during his journey to adulthood. He can face the world with excitement and a purpose to contribute positively to make the world a better place to live.

www.ingramcontent.com/pod-product-compliance
Lightning Source LLC
Chambersburg PA
CBHW072012070526
44583CB00015B/1453